This Is How We Do It

One Day in the Lives of Seven Kids from around the World

MATT LAMOTHE

chronicle books·san francisco

ITALY
My name is Romeo, and I'm called "Meo."
I'm eight years old.

JAPAN
My name is Kei, and I'm called "Kei-chan."
I'm nine years old.

UGANDA
My name is Daphine, and I'm called "Abwooli."
I'm seven years old.

RUSSIA
My name is Oleg, and I'm called "Olezhka."
I'm eight years old.

This
is me.

My name is Ribaldo, and I'm called "Pirineo."
I'm eleven years old.

INDIA
My name is Ananya, and I'm called "Anu."
I'm eight years old.

IRAN
My name is Kian.
I'm seven years old.

This is where I live.

RUSSIA

I live in a second-floor apartment in Uchaly, a <u>mining</u> town near the Ural mountains.

PERU

I live in a house my father built, in Los Naranjos, a village in the <u>Amazon rainforest</u>.

JAPAN

I live in a house in the metropolis of Tokyo, one of the largest cities in the world.

UGANDA
I live in a house made of <u>wood and mud</u>, in the village of Kanyawara.

ITALY
I live in a house in the village of Codrignano, with a <u>vineyard</u> in my backyard.

IRAN
I live in a second-floor apartment in the city of Gorgan, close to the <u>Caspian Sea</u>.

INDIA
I live in a first-floor apartment in the northern city of Haridwar, along the fast-flowing <u>Ganges River</u>.

IRAN

I live with my mom, Mahsa,
my dad, Mohammad, and my
little brother, Aran.

INDIA

I live with my mom, Shivi,
my dad, Mohit, and my
younger sister, Anika.

JAPAN

I live with my mom, Yuki,
my dad, Dai, and my
younger sister, Nao.

ITALY

I live with my mom, Francesca,
my dad, Oscar, my big brother, Ugo,
and my older sister, Mila.

This is who I live with.

PERU

I live with my mom, Sofía, my dad, Isaías, my younger brothers, Neyser and Eber, and my little sister, Neida. I also have four older siblings who don't live with us.

UGANDA

I live with my mom, Beatrace, my dad, Peter, and my older brother, Roger.

RUSSIA

I live with my mom, Katya, my dad, Albert, and my younger brother, Artem.

JAPAN

I choose my own clothes for school.
I like striped dresses and fancy socks.

IRAN

I wear a uniform that has a jacket
with a built-in shirt collar.

ITALY

I wear different clothes every day, but
my favorite is the dinosaur sweater.

PERU

We don't have a uniform.
I usually wear trousers, a T-shirt,
and a belt with a lion buckle.

This is what I wear to school.

INDIA

My uniform includes a special ID card I wear like a necklace.

RUSSIA

Boys are required to wear a black suit, white shirt, and tie, but I get to pick out the socks.

IRAN

I have *Barbari* bread, eggs, feta cheese, walnuts, and tea with sugar.

This is what I eat for breakfast.

UGANDA

I have *matoke* with meat, bread, eggs, and milk.

PERU

I have fried rice with chicken and peppers, sliced boiled plantains, and hot milk.

ITALY
I have toast with <u>Nutella</u> spread,
a cup of egg yolks mixed with
sugar and milk, and tea.

RUSSIA
I have oat <u>kasha</u>
with milk and
butter, <u>farmer</u>
<u>cheese</u>, bread,
and apple juice.

JAPAN
I have rice with *furikake*,
<u>miso</u> soup, grilled cod,
and an orange wedge.

INDIA
I have *paneer paratha* with
tomato chutney, and milk.

This is how
I go to school.

JAPAN

I walk by myself along the city streets past houses and shops. I smell roasting coffee beans from a café and say "*Ohayo gozaimasu*" to the crossing guards.

RUSSIA

I walk past large apartment buildings, a mosque, a church, cats basking in the sun, and <u>Mount Iremel</u>, far in the distance.

PERU

I walk next to the main road with my younger brothers and sister, sometimes stopping to buy a snack of sweet bread from a fruit stand.

IRAN

My mom or dad drives me in our car. We zoom past construction sites, office buildings, and people going to work.

ITALY

I ride a school bus past rivers and canyons, grape and olive fields, sometimes spotting a shepherd and his sheep.

UGANDA

I walk for half an hour with friends along a path, past bicyclists and groves of eucalyptus and banana trees.

INDIA

My mom drives me and my friends in a van through busy streets, past hotels, shops, and cows that freely roam the roads.

This is my teacher.

UGANDA
I call my teacher "Evelyn."
She's been teaching
for 8 years.

INDIA
I call my teacher "Aarti Bathla Ma'am."
She's been teaching for 4 years.

RUSSIA
I call my teacher
"Svetlana Anatolyevna."
She's been teaching
for 36 years.

PERU

I call my teacher
"Professor Pedro."
He's been teaching
for 26 years.

JAPAN

I call my teacher "*Sensei*."
She's been teaching
for 12 years.

ITALY

I call my teacher "Luisa."
She's been teaching for 20 years.

IRAN

I call my teacher
"*Khanoom Moalem*."
She's been teaching
for 6 years.

INDIA

We study <u>general awareness</u> and <u>value education</u> as well as subjects like math, Hindi, and English.

JAPAN

We all wear white indoor slippers and are in charge of cleaning our classroom every day. We study <u>ethics</u> as well as math, science, and Japanese.

This is how we learn.

PERU

Our school is very small, so the
fourteen kids in the fifth and sixth
grades study in the same room.
We have different subjects each day,
and our school ends at one o'clock.

RUSSIA

I study three languages: Russian, English, and Bashkir. I'm in a class with the same kids and the same teacher from first through fourth grades.

UGANDA

I study at a private school far from home, so I stay with my grandma, who has a house nearby. There are 69 boys and girls in my class, and we study math, reading, writing, and religion.

IRAN

I go to an all-boys school. We study reading and writing in Farsi, math, science, and the Quran.

ITALY

We do many activities outside the classroom, like visit parks and forests, go to museums in other cities, and put on a musical at the end of the year. We have school from eight o'clock to four o'clock.

This is how I spell my name.

RUSSIA
I write in Russian,
using the Cyrillic alphabet.

IRAN
I write in Farsi,
using the Persian alphabet.

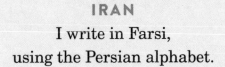

PERU
I write in Spanish,
using the Latin alphabet.

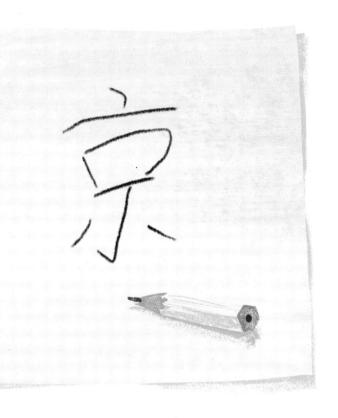

JAPAN
I write in Japanese,
using kanji characters.

UGANDA
I write in Rutooro and English,
using the Latin alphabet.

INDIA
I write in Hindi,
using the Devanagari alphabet.

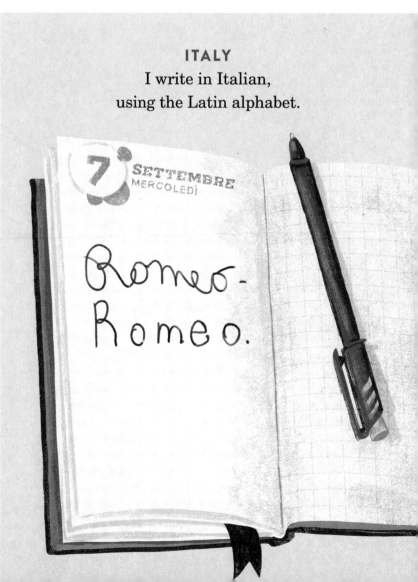

ITALY
I write in Italian,
using the Latin alphabet.

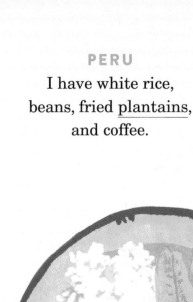

PERU

I have white rice, beans, fried <u>plantains</u>, and coffee.

IRAN

I have *adas polo*, fresh greens and herbs, salad (with tomato, cucumber, onion, and lime juice), and water.

INDIA

I have <u>chapati</u>, okra, a chocolate cookie, and water.

RUSSIA

I have barley <u>kasha</u> with butter, an open-faced sandwich with cheese, and tea with sugar.

This is what I eat for lunch.

JAPAN
I have rice with <u>chicken *katsu*</u>, soup (with cucumber, tofu, and seaweed), salad, and milk.

ITALY
I have ravioli with <u>sage</u> and cheese, and water.

UGANDA
I have *matoke* with tomato sauce, and water.

This is how I play.

UGANDA
I like to jump rope with
friends from school.

ITALY
I have rock-throwing contests in the hills behind my house.

RUSSIA
I play hockey with my team almost every day after school.

INDIA
I gather with all my friends in the park to play <u>Rumaal Chor</u> or "Hanky Thief."

JAPAN
I play <u>Koori Oni</u>, or "Freeze Tag," with friends on the playground by my house.

IRAN

I go horseback riding with my friends at a nearby stable.

PERU

I play soccer with my two brothers and nephew on a field by the main road.

This is how
I help.

UGANDA
I sweep the courtyard
with a broom.

INDIA
I hang wet laundry on
clotheslines to dry.

ITALY
I feed our four cats and some wild
ones that come to the backyard.

PERU
I help tend the cornfields
on our family farm.

RUSSIA
I vacuum
the floors
and rugs.

IRAN
I help take care of my little brother.

JAPAN
I help cook
dinner.

IRAN

On weekends we all have dinner together, but on weekdays it's just my mom, little brother, and me. We eat in the kitchen around nine o'clock, a dinner of grilled chicken, salad (with tomato and cucumbers), yogurt, and bread, with water to drink.

RUSSIA

We all eat together in the kitchen around six o'clock, a meal of salad, mashed potatoes, _kotleti_ with cheese sauce (my favorite), and bread. For dessert, my mom serves _oladi_ with condensed milk, cookies, and black tea.

This is how
we eat dinner.

ITALY

Sometimes during the week my family eats separately, but we always eat together on the weekends. We gather at the kitchen table around eight o'clock to eat lasagna with ragù Bolognese and béchamel sauce. We drink peach iced tea and water.

UGANDA

My brother, mom, housemaid, and I usually eat dinner around ten o'clock at night at our big wooden table. We have *matoke* with g-nut sauce, and milk to drink.

JAPAN

I eat with my parents and little sister in the dining room around seven o'clock. Our typical meal is fried salmon with tartar sauce, rice, salad (with apples, cucumbers, and tuna), tofu, miso soup, and milk or water to drink.

INDIA

My whole family eats together around nine o'clock in our dining room. We have chutney, carrots and potatoes, chapati, and yogurt, with water to drink.

PERU

My entire family gathers around seven o'clock to eat a dinner of white rice, boiled yuca, and stewed chicken, with coffee to drink.

RUSSIA
I play chess
with my dad.

This is what I do in the evening.

INDIA
My sister and I
play a board game
called Carrom.

UGANDA
I relax with
my family.

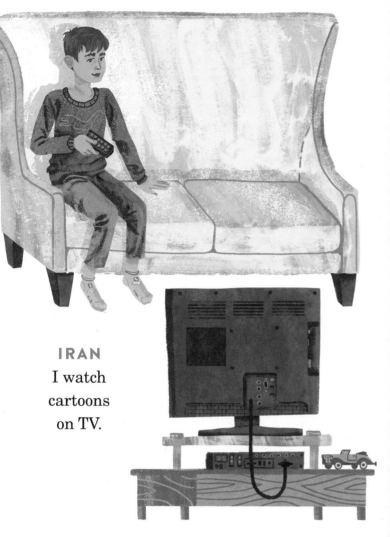

IRAN
I watch cartoons on TV.

PERU
I help my brother with his homework.

ITALY
I work on model cars with my dad.

JAPAN
My mom and I read mystery books together.

PERU
I sleep on wood planks with three folded blankets for padding, next to my sister.

ITALY
I sleep in my own room, on a wooden bed with a down blanket I use only during the winter.

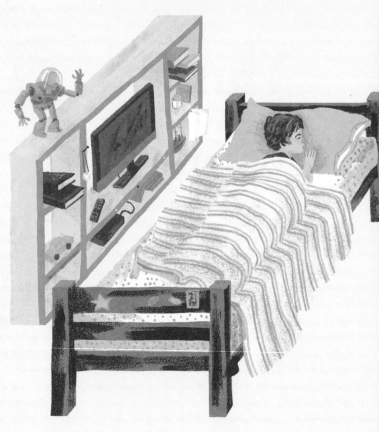

IRAN
I sleep in my own room, on a wooden bed with my favorite blanket.

JAPAN
I sleep on a <u>futon</u> on the floor, next to my sister.

This is where I sleep.

INDIA
I sleep on a huge bed, next to my sister and parents.

RUSSIA
I sleep on a lofted bed, in a room I share with my younger brother.

UGANDA
I sleep on a wooden bed, under a mosquito net, in a room I share with my parents.

This is my
night sky.

INDIA

IRAN

ITALY

JAPAN

PERU

MEET THE FAMILIES

This book follows seven real kids from around the world as they go about their typical day. They might be eating breakfast or playing outside while you're reading this very sentence!

We looked for families who have lived in the same country for generations. They follow many of the traditions unique to where they are from, but that doesn't mean the millions of people who call those same countries home have exactly the same tastes and experiences. Not everyone in Peru likes to play soccer, and not everyone in Japan eats fish for breakfast, in the same way that you and your friends may have to do different chores, and may wear different clothes.

While none of these kids can be representative of their country or culture, this genuine glimpse into their daily lives can reveal wonderful insights about lifestyles and traditions that may differ from our own.

UGANDA

RUSSIA

GLOSSARY

Abwooli means "catlike, caring, and feminine" in Rutooro, one of the native languages spoken in Uganda. It's one of twelve typical "pet names" given to kids shortly after birth, based on their personality.

Adas polo is an Iranian dish made with rice, lentils, onions, raisins, and spices, served vegetarian or with ground beef.

The Amazon rainforest is the largest and most biodiverse tropical rainforest in the world, covering 2.3 million square miles (3.7 million square kilometres) of land in South America. It contains 15,000 different species of trees, 1,000 bird species, and 2,200 fish species.

Barbari bread is a thick Iranian flatbread typically eaten with salty cheeses like feta.

Bashkir is a language related to Turkish. It is spoken by about 1.2 million Russians, many of whom live in the Bashkortostan Republic near the Ural Mountains.

Béchamel is a French white sauce made from butter, flour, and milk.

Carrom is a table game similar to billiards, where the objective is to flick disks into the four corner pockets.

The Caspian Sea is located between Europe and Asia and is considered to be the largest inland body of water.

Chapati is unleavened flatbread. The name comes from "chapat," which means "slap" in Hindi, because the bread can be made by slapping the dough between the palms.

Chicken katsu is a breaded, deep-fried chicken cutlet.

Ethics is a subject taught in Japan that encourages students to think about moral values like honesty, sincerity, fairness, equality, and justice.

Farmer cheese is pressed cottage cheese.

Furikake seasoning is usually sprinkled on top of rice, and may contain dried and ground fish, sesame seeds, chopped seaweed, sugar, salt, and MSG.

A futon is a flat mattress that in Japan is typically put away during the day and laid on the floor on top of a straw mat at night.

The Ganges River flows through northern India and Bangladesh and is the most sacred river for Hindus.

General awareness is a subject taught in India that includes lessons about the culture, geography, and politics of different countries.

G-nut is short for groundnut or a variety of peanut. In traditional Ugandan cooking it is ground and boiled to create a sauce typically served over a starch.

Khanoom Moalem means "Mrs. Teacher" in Persian.

Kasha means "porridge" in Russian and describes any type of grain boiled in water or milk.

Koori Oni is a Japanese version of Freeze Tag, in which kids tagged by the person who's "it" pretend they are frozen and stand with their arms crossed. If any player tags them again, they melt and can move.

Kotleti are pan-fried cutlets or croquettes made out of minced meat, bread soaked in milk, onions, and garlic.

Matoke is a nonsweet variety of banana, sometimes called a cooking banana. The fruit is picked while it's still green, then steamed and mashed.

Mining is the process of extracting valuable minerals, metals, and gems from the earth, either from the surface or from underground.

Miso soup is a traditional Japanese soup made with fish stock and miso paste (made with fermented soybeans and salt) as the base. A variety of ingredients can be added to the broth, most commonly tofu and seaweed.

Mount Iremel, at 5,200 feet (1,585 metres) high, is the highest peak in the Southern Ural Mountains.

Nutella is a sweet hazelnut-chocolate spread made by the Italian company Ferrero.

Ohayo gozaimasu means "good morning" in Japanese.

Oladi are Russian mini-pancakes traditionally made with fermented milk, which gives them a tangy flavor.

Paneer paratha is an Indian flatbread stuffed with cottage cheese and fried in oil.

Plantains are a starchier and less sweet variety of banana, typically eaten cooked. They can be fried, boiled, or baked.

Quran means "the recitation" in Arabic. It is the most important religious text for people of Islamic faith and is believed to have been spoken by God to the prophet Muhammad.

Ragù Bolognese is a meat-based sauce named for the town of Bologna, Italy. It's typically made with tomatoes, onion, celery, carrot, and ground beef (and sometimes pork), which simmer for a long time to create a thick sauce.

Rumaal Chor means "Hanky Thief" in Hindi, and is a variation on the American game Duck, Duck, Goose. The "thief" secretly drops a handkerchief behind one of the players seated in a circle, while the group sings a song. Once the hanky is found, that player chases the thief, who tries to get to the vacant seat before being caught.

Sage is an herb often used in Italian cooking. A member of the mint family, it has leaves that are very aromatic and have a musty, yet sweet flavor.

Sensei means "teacher" in Japanese and is how students address their teacher.

Svetlana Anatolyevna is an example of the way Russian kids typically address their elders, using their first name and patronymic (a variation on the father's name—in this case, Anatoli).

Value education is a subject taught in parts of India that includes lessons in basic manners and moral values.

A vineyard is a plantation of grapevines, typically grown for making wine, and sometimes grown for raisins.

A wood and mud house is traditional in Uganda. It's made by creating a structure of wood poles set 2 feet (61 centimetres) apart, with smaller reeds in between, that is then filled in with mud that dries and creates the walls. It is normally covered with a metal roof. The homes typically last 10 to 15 years.

Yuca, also known as cassava in English, is a long, tapered root vegetable containing large quantities of starch. It can be cooked and mashed or made into a flour.

AUTHOR'S NOTE

While walking in the jungle during a trip to Uganda, our guide told us to listen for elephants: "If you hear one, turn around quickly and walk away as fast as you can. Those guys are dangerous." We then went back to talking about our favorite phone apps.

I was amazed at both how different and how similar Uganda was from where I lived. I had many experiences in common with the people I met (like goofing off in class and hoping the teacher wouldn't see). I also heard stories of experiences I couldn't have dreamed of (like baboons making a mess in your house if you didn't lock your windows).

The world is a huge place inhabited by millions and millions of people who go through their lives doing the things they are used to, typically unaware of the daily activities of someone who lives in a country far away. I believe the more you learn about different people, the more you see yourself in them, and the more accepting you become. The more I thought about this, the more I wanted to compare and contrast moments in the lives of children from around the world. I hope to surprise readers with similiarities between us, as well as teach readers about the things we do completely differently.

With the help of friends (and friends of friends of friends) and family, I found seven children who agreed to share their day for this book. I put together a guide with detailed instructions about the photos and information I needed to fill each section of the book. Some of the families didn't speak English, so I enlisted help to translate the instructions into different languages. The families took pictures of their real breakfasts, homes, classrooms, and families. We communicated mostly through email, and sometimes messaging apps. I then used the photos as references to create all the illustrations you see in this book.

Matt Lamothe

the author MATT

Chicago,
USA

ROMEO

Codrignano,
Italy

DATE DUE

DAPHINE

Kanyawara,
Uganda